FIESTA!

CANADA

GROLIER

An Imprint of Scholastic Library Publishing
Danbury, Connecticut

Published for Grolier
an imprint of Scholastic Library Publishing
Old Sherman Turnpike, Danbury, Connecticut 06816
by Marshall Cavendish Editions
an imprint of Marshall Cavendish International
1 New Industrial Road, Singapore 536196

Set ISBN: 0-7172-5788-6
Volume ISBN: 0-7172-5790-8

Library of Congress Cataloging-in-Publication Data
Canada.
p. cm.—(Fiesta!)
Summary: Discusses the festivals and holidays of Canada and how the songs, food,
and traditions associated with these celebrations reflect the culture of the people.
1. Festivals—Canada—Juvenile literature. 2. Canada—Social life and customs—Juvenile literature.
[1. Festivals—Canada. 2. Holidays—Canada. 3. Canada—Social life and customs.]
I. Grolier (Firm). II. Fiesta! (Danbury, Conn.)
GT4813.A2C35   2004
394.2671—dc21   2003044843

For this volume
Author: Leena Ng
Editors: Krisinder Kaur
Designer: Ang Lee Ming
Production: Nor Sidah Haron
Crafts and Recipes produced by Stephen Russell

Printed by Everbest Printing Co. Ltd

Adult supervision advised for all crafts and recipes,
particularly those involving sharp instruments and heat.

CONTENTS

CANADA:

Canada is the second largest country in the world, smaller in area only than Russia. The name "Canada" comes from the Iroquois word "kanata," which means "village."

ALASKA

Northwest Territories

Yukon

Nunavut

PACIFIC OCEAN

British Columbia

Hudson Bay

Alberta

Manitoba

Saskatch- ewan

Ontario

Vancouver

Calgary

UNITED STATES

▲ **Hockey** is a major sport in Canada. It unites the country's different cultures in the cold climate. Former astronaut Marc Garneau even took a hockey puck and stick on his first voyage into space, in 1984.

▲ The **maple leaf** is a Canadian symbol. It appears on all Canadian coins and the flag. Canada's aboriginal peoples were the first to discover that sap from the maple tree could be made into food.

▲The **Niagara Falls** are a breathtaking view on the border between Ontario in Canada and New York in the United States. Many couples visit the falls on their honeymoon, and some people have tried to cross the falls on a tightrope or plunge down in a barrel.

GREENLAND (Denmark)

ATLANTIC OCEAN

Newfoundland

Quebec

OTTAWA

New Brunswick

Prince Edward Island

Nova Scotia

Montreal

Toronto

▶ **Mounties** enforce federal laws and provide police services in many provinces, towns, and native communities across Canada. Mounties also participate in international peacekeeping operations.

RELIGIONS

Most Canadians are either Roman Catholic or Protestant. These religions reached Canadian shores with early explorers from France and England. The Frenchman Samuel de Champlain founded Quebec City in 1608.

Saint Jean de Brébeuf is an important figure in Canadian religious history. Many schools in Canada are named after him.

ROMAN CATHOLICS in Canada are mostly of French descent and make up around 46 percent of the population. The Roman Catholic Church is the oldest Christian church in the world and has its headquarters in Rome in Italy. The first Roman Catholic missionaries settled in Canada in the 1600s, and in the 1700s Irish immigrants added to the Roman Catholic influence in Canada.

Canada's patron saint is Saint Jean de Brébeuf, a Jesuit missionary who did some great things in the country and yet is not well known in Canadian culture. Born in 1593 in Normandy in France, he grew up to be a Roman Catholic priest in the Jesuit order. In 1625 Brébeuf came to the New World with the French explorer Samuel de Champlain and worked among the Huron Indians in Quebec.

In 1649 Iroquois Indians, at war with the Huron Indians, captured the village of Brébeuf's Jesuit mission. The Iroquois Indians tortured Brébeuf to death.

Today Canadians recognize Brébeuf as a saint and martyr because of his many heroic deeds during his missionary life — he died for the sake of his religious beliefs. In 1930 the Roman Catholic Church canonized (officially declared as saints) Brébeuf and seven other Jesuits, known as the Jesuit Martyrs of North America. Roman Catholics in Canada and around the world remember these eight martyrs especially on October 19, their feast day.

PROTESTANTS make up around 36 percent of the population and are mostly English speakers. Canada's Protestants belong to several churches, such as the United Church of Canada, the Anglican Church, and the Lutheran Church.

MINORITY RELIGIONS in Canada include Judaism and a few Orthodox churches. Canada is like a jigsaw puzzle: Its citizens form a nation while keeping their cultural identities, complete with their languages, customs, and traditions. Apart from several European and Asian minority groups, Canada's aboriginal, or native, peoples — including the Inuit and the Indians — make up a very small part of the national population.

GREETINGS FROM **CANADA!**

English and French are Canada's two official languages although the province of New Brunswick is the only officially bilingual area in the country. However, most maps, brochures, and product labels in Canada are in both English and French. For the most part the French spoken in Canada is not identical to the language of France. In the province of Quebec, where the majority of the population is of French descent, the local tongue is known as Quebecois. However, most Quebeckers understand formal French.

How do you say...

Good morning/Good evening
Bonjour/Bonsoir

How are you?
Comment allez vous?

Please
S'il vous plait

Thank you
Merci

Goodbye
Au revoir

WINTER SOLSTICE

Celebrated for thousands of years by the Indians, the winter solstice continues to be significant for many Canadians as a day of hope and renewal.

I n Canada and the rest of the northern hemisphere December 21 is known as the winter solstice. It is the first day of the winter season and is also the shortest day of the year. This means that the time from sunrise to sunset on this day is shorter than on any other day in the year since the sun is at its lowest position in the sky on the day of the winter solstice.

Because the Earth is slightly tilted, the rays of the sun fall on Canada at an angle, and that leads to colder and shorter days during winter as the Earth turns on its axis.

Canadians celebrate the winter solstice with family and friends over a dinner of hot roast and mead (an alcoholic drink made from honey and water). They talk about their resolutions for the coming year. Some of the mead is poured on the ground as an offering.

The snowman Bonhomme is the king of winter carnival festivities.

During Canada's winter carnivals people go to grand balls wearing colorful masks like the one on the left. The carnival queen wears a crown like the one above in a grand ceremony at the start of the ball.

This day also starts the countdown to Christmas in Canada. Cities such as Quebec and Ottawa hold winter carnivals in the month of February.

The summer solstice, which falls on June 21, is also an important day for the aboriginal peoples. It is National Aboriginal Day. The winter solstice is special because it marks a new beginning, a time of renewal and the start of new things.

The solstices and the equinoxes (in March and September when day and night are equally long) are celebrated not only in Canada but throughout the world from England to China.

Ancient peoples made their own "clocks" and "calendars" out of stone to tell the time of day and to record the passing of the solstices and equinoxes during each year. One ancient "clock" was the sundial. It cast different shadows on the ground at different times of the day.

MAKE A SUNDIAL

YOU WILL NEED
Scissors
1 black card 11 by 9 inches
Pencil
1 gray card 11 by 9 inches
2 ice-cream sticks
Black crayon
Craft glue

1 Cut a square 9 inches by 9 inches from the black card. Put a plate face down on the gray card, and draw a circle. Cut out the circle, and lightly rub the side of the crayon on the circle to give it a worn look. Then glue the circle to the square to form the base of the sundial.

2 Make a small cut in one of the sticks a third of the way down from one end. Bend the stick at the cut, being careful not to break it, to form the L-shaped part of the pointer. Make two cuts in the other stick, each cut a quarter of the way down from each end. Fold the stick at the cuts to form the diagonal frame of the pointer, and glue it to the L shape.

3 Put the pointer on some leftover gray paper, and trace the outline on the paper. Cut along the outline, and shade it with the crayon. Then glue it to the sticks.

4 Using the crayon, draw 12 marks around the edge of the base circle. Put the pointer standing in the center of the base. Your sundial is ready! Watch the shadow of the pointer move from one mark to the next.

9

NATIONAL ABORIGINAL DAY

National Aboriginal Day celebrates Canada's native peoples, who have shared their land and culture with all Canadians. It is a day to give thanks for all that the native peoples have done for the nation.

A totem pole represents an Indian tribe or family. The poles are carved out of cedar wood.

June 21 is National Aboriginal Day in Canada. Since 1996 Canadians have set aside this day every year to show their respect and gratitude for the Indian, Inuit, and Métis peoples.

June 21 is also the summer solstice, or the longest day of the year. Canada's Indians have celebrated their culture and heritage around this date for generations.

The Indians are often called the First Nations. Many of Canada's cities are less than a hundred years old, but the Indians have lived on the land for centuries. They were the first people to explore the lakes, rivers, forests, and prairies. They helped the European immigrants to settle, teaching them how to find food, medicine, and clothing for survival and canoes and snowshoes for getting around.

Even today the native peoples still contribute to Canadian society. Their work in many areas, from the environment to the arts, have helped shape the culture and build the nation of Canada.

Indian chiefs wear headdresses made from eagle feathers. Each feather in the headdress is a prize that the chief got for a brave deed he did in the past.

The Indians hang dream catchers over their beds to protect them from nightmares and bring sweet dreams instead.

everyone. Powwows, for example, are big events when large numbers of people gather to enjoy one another's company and celebrate their culture and heritage. There is dancing, singing, food, storytelling, art displays, games, and horse races. Powwows are a tradition among native peoples across North America. They were originally held to give thanks after a hunt or a battle, to honor dead relatives, or to celebrate a special occasion in the community.

Other activities for the day include lacrosse matches (a ball-and-stick team sport), canoe races, trail rides, bake fairs, and demonstrations for making bannock bread.

Nonaboriginal people also participate in the celebrations on National Aboriginal Day, and this promotes understanding among the different races and cultures of Canada. Members of the aboriginal community organize and perform many ceremonies and activities to make it a fun and exciting day for

The aboriginal peoples living on the plains made their own bows and arrows for hunting animals.

MAKE A PICTURE ROBE

The First Nations recorded stories of battles, horse raids, and other major events by drawing pictures on animal hides. They then wore these hides as robes. You can make your own picture robe using some brown paper. Use your imagination to tell your own story in pictures.

YOU WILL NEED

1 large sheet brown wrapping paper
Pencil
Scissors
Crayons
Old string

1 Using the pencil, draw a shape like the one on the right on the brown wrapping paper. Cut out the shape, and crumple the paper to make it look like leather.

2 Spread the crumpled paper flat, and use the crayons to draw your pictures. (Draw on the rough side of the paper, not the shiny side.) You can draw pictures of nature (such as mountains, rivers, plants, and animals) or shapes such as stars and diamonds. Cover the paper with pictures.

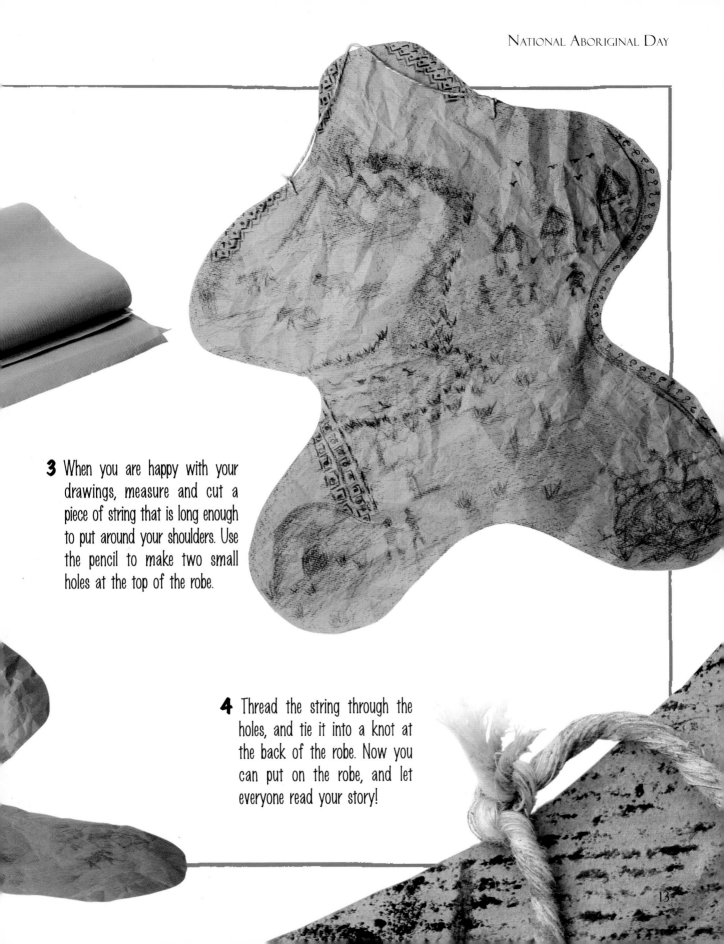

3 When you are happy with your drawings, measure and cut a piece of string that is long enough to put around your shoulders. Use the pencil to make two small holes at the top of the robe.

4 Thread the string through the holes, and tie it into a knot at the back of the robe. Now you can put on the robe, and let everyone read your story!

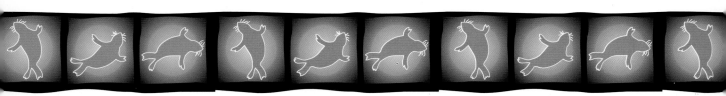

STORIES FROM THE SEA

*Many Inuit stories are connected to the sea. Here are two such stories:
one about Sedna, the sea spirit; the other about Kiviuk, who meets
many people and strange creatures as he crosses the sea.*

SEDNA was a young girl. One day a man asked her to marry him. She agreed and went to live with him. But Sedna later found that her husband was not a man but a fulmar (a bird similar to a gull) disguised as a man.

Sedna tried to leave with her father in his boat, but the fulmar flapped his wings so hard that a storm began. In fear Sedna's father tried to throw her to her husband, but she held onto the boat.

Then her father cut off her fingers, and Sedna fell into the sea. Her fingers turned into seals and other sea animals. It is said that ever since Sedna has lived at the bottom of the ocean with all the animals that were born from her fingers.

KIVIUK was an Inuit who traveled across the North Pole. Stories of his adventures are told throughout the Arctic, where he is known by many names, such as Qooqa and Qayaq. One story tells of Kiviuk's friendship with a boy. Everyone makes fun of the boy; Kiviuk is his only friend. Angered, the boy's grandmother tries to punish those who make fun of him. She turns him into a seal, and people follow him out to sea, hoping to catch a good meal for their families.

The boy's grandmother then starts a storm, and everyone who followed the seal drowns, except Kiviuk, safe in his kayak. The seal swims to shore, and his grandmother turns him back into a boy.

SAINT JEAN BAPTISTE DAY

Saint Jean Baptiste Day is a national holiday in Quebec. On this day Canadians in Quebec honor the province's patron saint, Saint Jean Baptiste (John the Baptist), with solemn ceremonies followed by lively festivities.

Saint Jean Baptiste Day falls on June 24. Canadians in Quebec and Montreal gather on this holiday to enjoy a traditional meal with family and friends and to light bonfires.

June 24 is a big feast day for Catholics all over the world, but especially so for those in France and Canada. The Feast of John the Baptist celebrates his birth not long before Jesus Christ was born more than 2,000 years ago. When John was older, he lived in the desert and preached about the coming of Jesus, and it was to John that Jesus went to be baptized in the Jordan River.

Early French settlers in Canada brought their traditions with them, and today people in Quebec and Montreal celebrate Saint Jean Baptiste Day every year with lively street processions.

Traditionally the day begins with Mass. One tradition on this day is the blessing of star- or heart-shaped loaves of bread called *petit pain*.

The festivities begin after Mass.

Marching bands, baton twirlers, and people in colorful costumes parade through the streets with banners and floats, amid singing and fiddle music. At sunset towns light a large bonfire in the town square, and there may also be fireworks displays.

It is recorded in the Bible that John the Baptist (left) announced the birth of Jesus (below) to the world.

PETIT PAIN

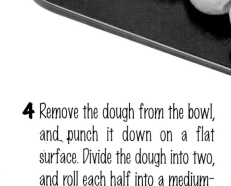

MAKES 2 LOAVES

1 cup warm water (115°F)
4½ tbsp dry yeast
2 tbsp sugar
⅓ cup softened margarine
1 tbsp salt
5 cups all-purpose flour
4 eggs
1 tbsp water
1 tbsp poppy seed (optional)

1 Pour half of the warm water into a large bowl. Sprinkle in the yeast, and stir until the yeast dissolves.

2 Add the remaining warm water, and the sugar, margarine, salt, and 1½ cups flour. Blend well. Stir in three eggs whole, one egg white (keep the yolk), and the remaining flour. Knead for 6 to 8 minutes, until smooth and elastic.

3 Put the dough in a greased bowl, cover, and allow to rise in a warm, draft-free place for 45 minutes, until the dough doubles in size.

4 Remove the dough from the bowl, and punch it down on a flat surface. Divide the dough into two, and roll each half into a medium-size rope.

5 Divide one rope into two equal pieces, and arrange them to form a heart. Divide the other rope into 10 equal pieces, and arrange them to form a star. Pinch the ends of the pieces together to seal the points of the heart and the star.

6 Cover the heart and the star with a thin cloth, and allow the loaves to rise in a warm, draft-free place for about 45 minutes.

7 Beat the remaining egg yolk with 1 tbsp water, and brush the loaves with the mixture. Sprinkle the poppy seed if desired. Bake at 400 degrees Farenheit for 20 minutes, turning over the loaves halfway through. Remove the loaves from the oven, and cool on wire racks.

CANADA DAY

On Canada Day people of different ethnic and cultural backgrounds celebrate their pride in being Canadian. After a day of barbecues, parades, and concerts fireworks fill the night sky.

On July 1 people all over Canada, whether in the cities, towns, or villages, celebrate their country's birthday. On this date in

People wear festive red-and-white paper party hats during the Canada Day celebrations.

1868 Governor General Lord Monck proclaimed the British provinces in North America united as one country, Canada. The four provinces were Nova Scotia, New Brunswick, Quebec, and Ontario, on the eastern side of North America. Six other British colonies were later added: Alberta, British Columbia, Manitoba, Newfoundland, Prince Edward Island, and Saskatchewan. In addition to the 10 provinces there are three territories in Canada: the Northwest Territories, Nunavut, and the Yukon Territory.

Each province and territory has its own team of volunteers to organize the local celebrations for Canada Day.

People from different ethnic backgrounds put on their traditional cultural dress for the street parades in the big cities. Afterward people go to the parks to watch concerts performed by local musicians and to taste food from the different cultures.

Cheerleaders dance with colorful pompoms during the street parades.

Canadians wave their national flag on Canada Day.

The biggest Canada Day party is in Ottawa, where the Canadian prime minister gives a speech on Parliament Hill. Other big cities such as Toronto and Vancouver also have big parties. Many people go to these parties wearing red-and-white paper hats with Canada's maple leaf symbol. There are also lots of activities for children, such as clown acts, magic shows, sack races, soapbox derbies, and face painting.

The day's celebrations end with a spectacular display of fireworks in the evening. Everyone looks forward to the fireworks, as they soak in their pride of calling Canada home.

MAPLE LEAF FOREVER

O land of blue un - en - ding skies, mount - ains strong and spark - ling snow. A scent of free - dom in the wind, o'er the em' - rald fields be - low. To thee we brought our hope, our dreams, for thee we stand to - ge - ther. Our land of peace, where proud - ly flies the Ma - ple leaf for - ev - ver.

CALGARY STAMPEDE

Agricultural fairs are held all over Canada during summer to celebrate the achievements of farmers and ranchers. The main attraction of the Calgary Stampede is its Wild West activities.

Every year in July more than a million people from around the world visit the city of Calgary in Alberta in western Canada for the Calgary Stampede. "The Greatest Outdoor Show on Earth," as the festival is known, began in 1912. It celebrates Western hospitality in the heart of the Canadian Rockies.

For 10 days the city of Calgary turns into a rodeo town with chuck-wagon races, bull-riding, and many other exciting events. The whole city feels the spirit of the Stampede: Coffeeshops serve pancake breakfasts with sausages, eggs, and hash browns; musicians play country music in the parks; and people square-dance in the streets.

A gigantic carnival features such favorites as ferris wheels and even a haunted house, and there is an Indian village so visitors can get close to aboriginal culture. Hotels, stores, restaurants, and banks are decorated with a Western motif, and the people dress as cowboys and cowgirls in jeans and cowboy boots.

Every afternoon during the Calgary Stampede the best cowboys from Canada and other countries saddle up and show off their skills in riding wild horses and handling cattle. The most dangerous event of the rodeo is the heart-stopping bull-riding race.

Chuckwagon racing is another contest of nerves and horsepower. Add to them a horse race, a cow-milking event, and rodeo clowns, and this becomes a Wild West experience few will ever forget.

Parade Day is the highlight of the Calgary Stampede. On Parade Day beautiful floats, marching bands, more than a thousand horses and cowboys, and a host of other features and activities entertain young and old alike.

Prize cattle and horses are paraded at the Calgary Stampede. Adults and children wear cowboy hats to get into the spirit of the Wild West.

BLUEBERRY PANCAKES

MAKES 6 PANCAKES

4 tbsp baking powder
2 cups flour
1 tbsp salt
1 tbsp cinnamon
¼ tsp vanilla
2 tbsp granulated sugar
1½ cups milk
4 eggs, separated
½ cup melted butter
1 cup frozen blueberries

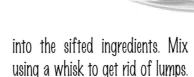

1 Sift the baking powder and flour together with the salt, cinnamon, vanilla, and sugar.

2 Combine the milk, egg yolks, butter, and blueberries, and stir into the sifted ingredients. Mix using a whisk to get rid of lumps.

3 Beat the egg whites until stiff and frothy. Then fold the egg whites into the batter a little at a time.

4 With the help of an adult pour the batter onto a hot, oiled griddle, about ⅓ cup at a time. Cook until the top of each pancake bubbles, then turn and cook the other side. Serve pancakes with maple syrup.

HERITAGE DAY

On Heritage Day Canadians explore and celebrate their cultural roots. They recall their country's history and reflect on the things that have made their nation what it is today.

Heritage Day is celebrated each year to honor the importance and beauty of Canada's heritage. The actual date it falls on varies from province to province, but generally the holiday is celebrated on the third Monday in February.

Heritage Day gives Canadians a time and place to celebrate their country's rich history and to try to understand and appreciate the cultures that have built Canada into a nation. By talking about people and events that have made a name for Canada in the world, Canadians can grow to understand what Canada stands for and what it means to them to be Canadian, and they can be thankful for God's blessing of a wonderful homeland.

Among many things that people can do on Heritage Day is to visit Canada's heritage sites. They include

the Rocky Mountains and several national parks, the old-town sections of the big cities, and ancient native burial sites.

There are so many places where people can look to learn more about Canada! There are books, television programs, and Internet sites describing everything and anything Canadian, from native inventions and stories, to copper and diamond mines, to world-famous

Canada's copper mines are part of its heritage. The aboriginal peoples mined copper to make tools, and today Canada is the world's largest exporter of copper.

musicians such as Shania Twain and Celine Dion.

Festivities are as much a part of celebrations on Heritage Day as they are of celebrations on any other big holiday: Local musicians, singers, and dancers entertain the crowds with concert after concert; booths offer a taste of different ethnic foods; and children take part in games and quizzes about their country.

The first canoes were made from birchbark wood and had animal carvings on them.

GREAT PEACE RIVER

There's a ri - ver that is flo-wing up to - ward the nor - thern sea; It's not famed in song or sto - ry, still it has a charm for me. It has called me from the south - land where the star - ry ban - ner blows, And I've set - tled down for - ev - er where the great Peace Ri - ver flows.

Canada's native peoples discovered how to make maple syrup from the sap of the maple tree.

THANKSGIVING

On Thanksgiving Day Canadians remember their ancestors who built the country. People recall how the pioneers lived and celebrate the importance of farming in Canada.

Thanksgiving Day is celebrated all over Canada on the second Monday of October every year. It is thought that this tradition began with the first European settlers.

Long ago farmers in Europe celebrated many harvest festivals. To thank God for healthy crops that gave them lots of food, they always had a goat's horn filled with plenty of fruit and grain on their dinner tables. When they came to North America, these European farmers brought this tradition.

But the first recorded Canadian Thanksgiving was celebrated in what is now Newfoundland in 1587. English explorer Martin Frobisher held a

It is believed that the Indians were the first to grow corn in North America.

grand ceremony there to give thanks to God for getting him through his voyage from England to Canada. (Frobisher Bay, off the northern coast of Canada, was named after Martin Frobisher.) Many who came after Frobisher gave thanks to God in the same way for their safe arrival in Canada.

The early French also held thanksgiving feasts in Canada. Starting with pioneers such as Jean de Brébeuf and Samuel de Champlain, they shared their food with the native peoples to show goodwill.

The early Americans also brought their own harvest celebrations to Canada. They held the

first of them in Nova Scotia. Americans loyal to England during the American Revolution left for Canada, where they spread their thanksgiving customs and practices.

Families in Canada celebrate Thanksgiving with a special dinner for family and friends. The dinner usually includes a roasted stuffed turkey and a pumpkin pie.

Turkey with cranberry sauce (below) is the main dish at any Thanksgiving dinner. Root vegetables such as parsnips and beets, and fruits such as grapes (above) are commonly served as side dishes.

25

CHRISTMAS

Christmas is one of the main religious festivals celebrated by Christians in Canada. During the Christmas season Canadians decorate their houses and yards with lights, put up Christmas trees, and exchange gifts and greeting cards.

C hristmas Day is celebrated all over the world on December 25 every year. Christians go to church on this day to remember the birth of Jesus Christ. In parts of Canada people also visit the crèche in church and set up their own nativity scenes at home. There may also be a procession with an icon of the baby Jesus.

Christmas is really a religious event, which Christians celebrate to remember with joy the coming of God to save

the world. People share this joy among friends and family at church and at home, and sing carols in the streets. Traditionally people also take the joy of Christmas to the less fortunate, such as the poor, the aged, and the sick, who have no one to look after them.

The Christmas tree is usually a tall pine tree; an evergreen, it represents life. In snowy countries such as Canada families take real pine trees into their homes and hang lights, balls, bells, bows, tinsel, and toys on the trees. Families also bake gingerbread cookies, a tradition originating in Germany. These cookies are often

shaped as houses with snow-covered rooftops and light-trimmed doors and windows.

On Christmas Eve children in Canada also hope for a midnight visit from Santa Claus. Santa is the American version of

Saint Nicholas, a bishop who lived in an area in present-day Turkey in the fourth century A.D. He was born to wealthy parents; but when he grew up, he sold off his inheritance in order to help the needy and the suffering.

The Christmas feast is one of the high points of this festive time. For many Catholics this is supper at home after the midnight Mass, although the feasting continues on Christmas Day. A truly homemade supper, lunch, or dinner takes days to prepare: roast turkey or beef, meat pies, mince pies, plum pudding, and a chocolate log cake decorated with the symbols of a white Christmas such as snowmen and sleds.

This gingerbread house is decorated with figures of Santa Claus, a snowman, and pine trees.

Candy canes (opposite) look a lot like a shepherd's crook, only they taste better.

The Christmas tree (right) almost always has a star on top. When Jesus was born, a bright star led shepherds and kings to his crib.

People usually open their presents when they come home from church. But children, too excited, may run to the tree or the stockings as soon as they wake up on Christmas morning to open the gifts that Santa Claus brought silently at night.

THE END OF WINTER

Christmas in Canada coincides with the winter solstice, an ancient festival.
The native peoples tell this story about how, after an endless winter,
the earth began a cycle of rebirth and new life with the four seasons.

ONCE THERE was a very long winter — the sun did not shine for years. With so much snow and so little food all the animals decided to find out where the earth's heat had gone. The mouse, lynx, fox, wolf, and pike (a kind of fish) went to the upper world in search of the heat.

After looking around for some time, the animals saw a campfire and a tepee (a Plains Indian tent) near a lake. Inside the tepee were two baby bears — their mother was out hunting — and three big bags. The wolf pointed at the first bag and asked the cubs, "What is in this bag?"

"That is where mommy keeps the rain," they said.

"And what is in this one?" the pike pointed at the second bag.

"That is where she keeps the wind."

"And this one?" the fox asked.

"That," the cubs whispered, "is where she keeps the heat."

"Aahh…," the visitors said and left.

Outside they found a place to hide.

"How are we going to get the bag of heat?" they asked one another. They decided to distract the mother bear when she came back to the tepee so that they could take the bag without her knowing.

The lynx ran to the other side of the lake and changed into a deer; the mouse gnawed into the bear's paddle; and the others hid near the tepee.

Soon the mother bear returned. She saw the deer across the lake and jumped into her canoe. She was some distance away from the shore when the paddle broke where the mouse had gnawed it.

The other animals ran into the tepee and took the bag of heat. Then they ran with the bag to the door that led out of the upper world. The bag broke, and all the heat escaped and spread throughout the world below. The ice melted, rivers flowed again, trees sprouted leaves, and flowers bloomed.

That is how the world got its seasons, spring always following winter.

LOBSTER CARNIVAL

During the lobster season from May to July Canadian port towns on the Atlantic coast bustle with lobster feasts. The best known among them is the Summerside Lobster Carnival.

Summerside, a town on the western side of Prince Edward Island, gets very busy in summer. Come July every year the normally quiet seaside town begins its well-known Summerside Lobster Carnival.

Canadians living in Summerside had their first big lobster carnival more than 30 years ago. That was when they decided to set aside a day every year to honor and thank the local lobster catchers, who were important to many of the town's businesses.

Summerside's carnival was originally a one-day event to mark the end of the lobster season. People gathered to see the town's lobster catchers march in a parade and then compete for the "Fastest Lobster Boat" trophy in a race on the harbor.

Years later the carnival stretched into a week-long festival in July. Besides parades and boat races, the carnival now also has king lobster contests, lobster stews and salads, boat rides, fund-raising celebrity dinners, trap-making demonstrations, spelling bee and fiddle competitions, and many other exciting events.

Lobsters come in many colors, even green, and some have spotted shells. The American lobster has two fleshy, powerful claws, but most of its meat is in the tail.

WORDS TO KNOW

Aboriginal people: The original inhabitants of a country or region.

Bannock: A flat bread made from oat or barley flour.

Chuckwagon: A horse-drawn cart used by the North American pioneers for long-distance travel.

Colony: A group of people who leave their homeland and settle in a faraway country.

Crèche: A representation of the scene in the stable at Bethlehem when Jesus Christ was born.

Equinox: One of two times in a year when the length of day and night are the same. The vernal equinox takes place in March, the autumnal equinox in September.

Inuit: An Eskimo who lives in the Arctic.

Lacrosse: A Native American game played with two teams using long sticks with a net at the end to catch or throw a ball into the opponents' goal.

Lynx: A wildcat with long legs, a short tail, and bushy ears. It roams the forest mostly at night and is rarely seen by people.

Métis: A person of mixed Native American and French-Canadian ancestry.

Nativity: The birth of Jesus Christ, celebrated by Christians on December 25.

Powwow: A big gathering of Native Americans.

Rodeo: A sport that tests a cowboy's horseriding and cattle-roping skills.

Solstice: One of two times in a year when the sun is farthest from the equator.

Stampede: A celebration of the culture of the Wild West, with a rodeo, dancing, food, and contests.

Sundial: An instrument that shows the time of day by casting shadows on a plate.

ACKNOWLEDGMENTS

WITH THANKS TO:
Desmond Ng, Ng Swee Leng, Mohd Asyraf Bin Omar, R. Pramela, Senthamarai Rogawansamy, Eunice Sin, and Jena Yap for the loan of artifacts

PHOTOGRAPHS BY:
Haga Library, Japan (cover), Yu Hui Ying (p. 8 bottom left, p. 10 top left, p. 11 top left, p. 19 top left, pp. 24-25, p. 27 bottom left), Sam Yeo (all others)

ILLUSTRATIONS BY:
Ang Lee Ming (p. 1), Amy Ong (pp. 4-5), Cake (p. 7), Lee Kowling (p. 15), Ong Lay Keng (p. 29)

SET CONTENTS